Made in United States
Orlando, FL
16 December 2024

55901498R00065